INCREDIBLE ANIMAL LIFE CYCLES
LIFE CYCLE OF A
CHICKEN

by Karen Latchana Kenney

pogo

Ideas for Parents and Teachers

Pogo Books let children practice reading informational text while introducing them to nonfiction features such as headings, labels, sidebars, maps, and diagrams, as well as a table of contents, glossary, and index.

Carefully leveled text with a strong photo match offers early fluent readers the support they need to succeed.

Before Reading

• "Walk" through the book and point out the various nonfiction features. Ask the student what purpose each feature serves.

• Look at the glossary together. Read and discuss the words.

Read the Book

• Have the child read the book independently.

• Invite him or her to list questions that arise from reading.

After Reading

• Discuss the child's questions. Talk about how he or she might find answers to those questions.

• Prompt the child to think more. Ask: Have you ever seen a chick hatch from an egg? What other animals hatch from eggs?

Pogo Books are published by Jump!
5357 Penn Avenue South
Minneapolis, MN 55419
www.jumplibrary.com

Library of Congress Cataloging-in-Publication Data

Names: Kenney, Karen Latchana, author.
Title: Life cycle of a chicken / by Karen Latchana Kenney.
Description: Minneapolis, MN : Jump!, Inc., [2018]
Series: Incredible animal life cycles
Audience: Age 7-10. | Includes index.
Identifiers: LCCN 2017058878 (print)
LCCN 2017049637 (ebook)
ISBN 9781624968082 (ebook)
ISBN 9781624968068 (hardcover : alk. paper)
ISBN 9781624968075 (paperback)
Subjects: LCSH: Chickens—Life cycles—Juvenile literature.
Classification: LCC SF487.5 (print)
LCC SF487.5 .K46 2019 (ebook) | DDC 636.5—dc23
LC record available at https://lccn.loc.gov/2017058878

Editor: Jenna Trnka
Book Designer: Molly Ballanger

Photo Credits: irin-k/Shutterstock, cover (left); Tsekhminster/Shutterstock, cover (right); yevgeniy11/Shutterstock, 1; Sascha Burkard/Shutterstock, 3; saied shahin kiya/Shutterstock, 4; Anneka/Shutterstock, 5; SasaStock/Shutterstock, 6-7; Santirat Praeknokkaew/Shutterstock, 8-9; DenisNata/Shutterstock, 10; Sonia Cervantes/Shutterstock, 11; Nataly Studio/Shutterstock, 12-13; mar_chm1982/Shutterstock, 14-15; Chokniti Khongchum/Shutterstock, 16; Olexandr Panchenko/Shutterstock, 17; Vicki Vale/Shutterstock, 18-19; Chesh/Alamy, 20-21; Oleksandr Lytvynenko/Shutterstock, 23.

Printed in the United States of America at Corporate Graphics in North Mankato, Minnesota.

TABLE OF CONTENTS

CHAPTER 1
Just Hatched 4

CHAPTER 2
Growing into Chickens 10

CHAPTER 3
Making New Eggs 16

ACTIVITIES & TOOLS
Try This! 22
Glossary 23
Index 24
To Learn More 24

CHAPTER 1

JUST HATCHED

Peck, peck, peck. An egg begins to crack. Peck, peck, peck. The crack in the shell grows bigger.

A baby chick pushes its way out. Its feathers are wet. The little bird is just starting its life. It will grow and change during its life cycle.

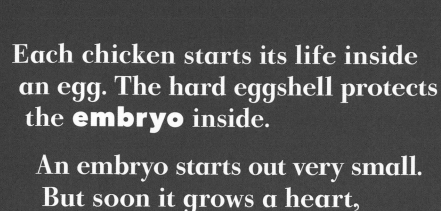

Each chicken starts its life inside an egg. The hard eggshell protects the **embryo** inside.

An embryo starts out very small. But soon it grows a heart, a beak, feathers, and more. It eats the egg **yolk** to grow.

DID YOU KNOW?

Eggshells are hard, but they have many tiny holes called **pores**. The pores let in air and water.

In about 20 days, the chick is big enough to break out of its egg. The baby chick uses its **egg tooth**. The egg tooth breaks the shell. After the chick **hatches**, the egg tooth falls off its beak.

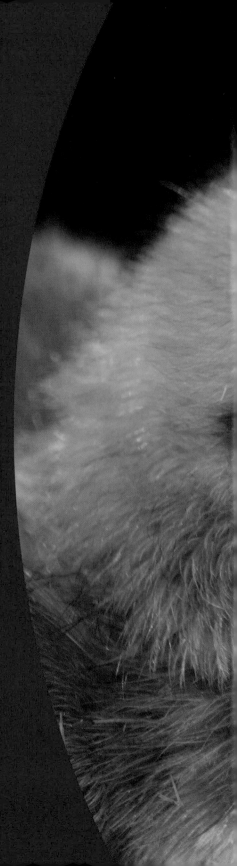

egg tooth

CHAPTER 2

GROWING INTO CHICKENS

Newly hatched chicks are tired and wet. They rest. Their downy feathers dry and fluff up.

New chicks in the wild find food. What do they eat? Seeds, insects, and berries. Chicks on farms eat **feed**. Their mother keeps them safe.

After a week, the chicks start to **molt**. They lose their downy feathers. Smooth feathers grow in their place. In about six weeks, the chicks are bigger. They need new feathers and molt again.

DID YOU KNOW?

Even adult chickens molt. They shed their feathers once a year.

Now the birds are adult chickens. A female is called a hen. A male is a rooster. These adults live in groups called **flocks**. Each flock has one rooster and 12 to 15 hens.

The flock lives, eats, and sleeps together. They **roost** above the ground when they sleep. It keeps them safe from **predators**.

rooster

hen

TAKE A LOOK!

Each chicken goes through a life cycle. It has three **stages**:

egg:
An embryo grows inside the egg for 20 to 21 days.

chick:
A chick takes between 18 to 25 weeks to grow into an adult.

adult:
An adult chicken can live 8 to 10 years.

CHAPTER 3

MAKING NEW EGGS

At four months old, hens can lay eggs. To make chicks, a rooster and hen **mate**. Embryos will grow inside the hen's eggs.

Not all of the eggs they lay have embyos. Those are picked by farmers. These are the eggs people eat.

A hen lays a **clutch** of eggs in a dry, soft spot. Each clutch has around 8 to 12 eggs.

Then the hen takes a break from laying eggs. She needs to make sure her eggs hatch.

DID YOU KNOW?

A hen is born with all the eggs she will lay in her life. She has several thousand of them in her body. They are tiny. They grow bigger when she is ready to lay them.

clutch

She sits on them to keep them warm. She takes good care of them.

Soon the chicks will hatch. They will start growing, too. Then they will start the life cycle all over again!

ACTIVITIES & TOOLS

TRY THIS!

EGGSHELL PORES

Try this activity to find the pores in eggshells.

What You Need:

- 2 eggs
- liquid dish soap
- food coloring (blue or green)
- water
- bowl
- measuring cup and spoons
- spoon
- cup
- paper towel

1. Pour 1½ cups of water into the bowl.

2. Add ¼ teaspoon dish soap and ¼ teaspoon food coloring to the water. Mix well.

3. Add eggs to the mixture. Make sure they are underwater. If they aren't, make and add more of the water mixture. Let the eggs soak one hour.

4. Remove the eggs from the mixture. Carefully crack the eggs over the cup. Try not to break the shells too much.

5. Place the shells on the paper towel. Look at the insides of the shells closely. What do you see? The colored dots show where the mixture went through the shell. This is where the pores are in the shell. When you are done, wash your hands well.

GLOSSARY

clutch: A group of eggs laid together.

egg tooth: A little spike on a chick's upper beak that the chick uses to break out of its shell.

embryo: An animal in the earliest stage of its life cycle.

feed: Special food that farmers give to chickens and other animals.

flocks: Groups of animals that live, eat, travel, and sleep together.

hatches: Breaks out of an egg.

mate: When a male and female animal come together to make babies.

molt: To shed old skin, feathers, or coverings.

pores: Tiny holes that let liquids or gases move through something, like an eggshell.

predators: Animals that hunt other animals for food.

roost: To settle somewhere to rest for the night.

stages: Steps or periods of development.

yolk: The yellow part of an egg that an embryo eats as it grows.

INDEX

adult chickens 13, 14, 15

beak 7, 8

chick 5, 8, 10, 11, 13, 15, 16, 21

clutch 18

egg 4, 7, 8, 15, 16, 17, 18

egg tooth 8

embryo 7, 15, 16, 17

farmers 17

feathers 5, 7, 10, 13

flocks 14

food 11

hatches 8, 10, 18, 21

hen 14, 16, 18

life cycle 5, 15, 21

mate 16

molt 13

peck 4

pores 7

predators 14

roost 14

rooster 14, 16

shell 4, 7, 8

stages 15

yolk 7

TO LEARN MORE

Learning more is as easy as 1, 2, 3.

1) **Go to www.factsurfer.com**

2) **Enter "lifecycleofachicken" into the search box.**

3) **Click the "Surf" button to see a list of websites.**

With factsurfer, finding more information is just a click away.